A
BOUQUET
FOR MOM

An Arrangement
of Stories, Meditations,
and Biblical Inspirations

SUSAN B. TOWNSEND

Adams Media
Avon, Massachusetts

Published by
Adams Media, an F+W Publications Company
57 Littlefield Street, Avon, MA 02322. U.S.A.
www.adamsmedia.com

ISBN: 1-59337-601-4

Printed in the United States of America.

J I H G F E D C B A

Library of Congress Cataloging-in-Publication Data
Townsend, Susan
A bouquet for mom : an arrangement of stories, meditations, and biblical inspirations
/ Susan Townsend.
p. cm.
ISBN 1-59337-601-4
1. Mothers--Religious life. 2. Mothers in the Bible--Meditations. I. Title.

BV4529.18.T69 2006
242'.6431--dc22
2005026047

This publication is designed to provide accurate and authoritative information with
regard to the subject matter covered. It is sold with the understanding that the
publisher is not engaged in rendering legal, accounting, or other professional advice.
If legal advice or other expert assistance is required, the services of a competent
professional person should be sought.
—From a *Declaration of Principles* jointly adopted by a Committee of the
American Bar Association and a Committee of Publishers and Associations

Many of the designations used by manufacturers and sellers to distinguish their
product are claimed as trademarks. Where those designations appear in this book and
Adams Media was aware of a trademark claim, the designations have been printed
with initial capital letters.

Interior photos © 2005 Brand X Photos and ©1996 PhotoDisc.

This book is available at quantity discounts for bulk purchases.
For information, please call 1-800-872-5627.

Dedication

In loving memory of my mother,
Barbara Armstrong, 1925–1989.

Acknowledgments

And because I can hear my mother saying, "Did you say thank-you?" I'd like to acknowledge…

Kate Epstein and the people at Adams Media for giving me this extraordinary opportunity.

Kirsten Amann for her enthusiasm and encouragement, as well as her invaluable assistance.

God, for answering my prayers and opening the door.

My pastor, Ted Petts, for urging me to walk through that door.

My dear friend, Martin, for pointing out the simple joys along the way.

Gabriel, Emily, Dylan, Connor, and Owen for being the best things that ever happened to me.

Thomas E., without whom the page would still be blank.

Contents

Preface

The Language of Flowers

For centuries, we've used flowers to send messages of love, hope, goodwill, and sympathy. Flowers have a language of their own, with each bloom carrying a distinctive meaning. Even in cultures as early as the Persian empire, flowers carried secret messages. A gardenia meant "I'm worshiping you in secret" and a yellow rose symbolized jealousy, infidelity, and bad luck. Victorian women carried small bouquets, called tussie-mussies, which conveyed secret messages in the language of the flowers. Strands of ivy signified fidelity and friendship, and gardenias conveyed a secret love.

Our bouquet for Mom must contain a myriad of blooms— a painter's palette of colors—to delight her senses and, most importantly, to tell her how we feel. We have so much to say, and the list is endless of things that make her special. We can use the language of flowers to convey a few of the feelings from our hearts and to share just a few of the many qualities that distinguish her as one of God's most special creations—a mom.

Chapter One
A Pot Marigold for Joy

With its wealth of blooms, the cheerful yellow-and-orange pot marigold is the perfect flower to represent the abundant joy in a mother's journey. Like the expanding, enduring happiness it represents, the pot marigold will appear in a garden year after year, increasing in number each time. Just as those first tiny shivers of delight hint at the multitude of blessings to come, the early buds on the small young marigolds herald the coming of a bounty of blossoms.

Joy

Find joy with your child in the simple things—a rainbow after a storm, a spider's web discovered in a doorway, an unexpected smile, and a joke that makes no sense. Watch your child and share the joy he feels in running, pretending, and printing his name for the first time. Listen to your child, and gain the wisdom that only mothers know. Talk to your child often, and always remember to say, "You are a gift from God. You make me happy."

Mary's Story

*"And Mary said, 'My soul doth magnify the Lord,
And my spirit hath rejoiced in God my Saviour.'"*

—Luke 1:46–47

Imagine Mary's delight, thousands of years ago, when her newborn son was first placed in her arms. This child was the Savior, born to take away the sin of the world, but her happiness on that night was no different than that of countless mothers in the history of the world. Like all mothers in those first moments after birth, she cradled his precious head and inhaled his intoxicating fragrance. She marveled at his tiny toes and his fingernails like miniature pearls. And she basked in the blessed warmth of their first hug.

There is an abundance of joy in motherhood—a profusion of happiness that begins long before the baby is born. This joy accompanies you on your amazing journey from woman to mother. It opens your heart to the miracle of unconditional love and renews your strength when exhaustion and despair strain your spirit. Mary, the mother of Jesus, knew this joy well. Like many of us, she faced the news of her pregnancy, first with astonishment and then with great happiness.

With movements as gentle as the flutter of butterfly wings, her baby made his first tentative introductions. As time passed, he stretched his arms and kicked his legs, a blessed reminder of the miraculous events about to occur. For Mary, these were moments of elation and amazement. A timeless bond was formed—new and fragile in those first few weeks, but strengthened with each passing day. And so, on these night she held her son for the first time, it wasn't the meeting of two strangers, but the joyful recognition of her heart's desire.

My First Mother's Day

Even though I've been a mother for close to twenty years and my family has done a wonderful job of making me feel wanted and needed every day of the year, I've never felt that Mother's Day has been about me. My own mother has been gone for almost sixteen years, but in my heart and mind, she has remained the guest of honor on that special day.

I know I'm a good mother. I also know that, if she were still living, my mother would be extremely proud of me. But there's a tiny part of me that still feels as though I've never quite filled her shoes. I suspect this doubt emerged after her death, as I moved forward through life without her unfailing support and encouragement. If she were still living, I'm quite sure she would be amused, and even a bit annoyed, by my fear that I haven't met her standards or reached her level of perfection and would have told me this was all a product of my vivid imagination. In any case, my mother would banish any doubts I had and comfort me as only a mother could.

Despite her absence, my mother still found a way to reassure me during our Mother's Day service at church yesterday. The pastor and his wife have always put a lot of effort into making this a memorable day for the mothers in the congregation, and I was certain this year would be enjoyable as well. What I didn't know was that a special effort had been put forth on my behalf.

One of the greatest blessings of my life is the fact that my five children have accepted Jesus as their personal Savior. The four youngest children have always attended church with their father and me every Wednesday evening and Sunday morning, but our oldest boy, Gabe, has never joined us. While I've rejoiced in his salvation, I've longed for the day when all my children went to church. We've invited him many, many times, but his answer has never changed. I've prayed about it a great deal and, for the most part, accepted that this was something that would happen in God's time. This was not a dream that would come true by force.

On the morning of Mother's Day, we took our regular seats in the second pew from the front, and the service commenced in the usual manner, with hymns, announcements, and members of the congregation sharing blessings and prayer requests. The pastor read some humorous comments made by second-grade children responding to questions about their mothers, and then he announced that, once again, this year, he was going to ask the children to talk about their mothers. He looked to the back of the church and said, "Gabriel, would you like to start?"

Unable to believe what I had just heard, I whirled around in my seat and stared. There he was—my six-foot, 185-pound firstborn—sitting in the last pew, looking a little self-conscious, but obviously pleased with himself. I burst into tears and grinned at the same time. I turned to my husband, Tom, unable to contain my excitement. "He's here! Do you see him? He's here! Did you know about this?"

Tom smiled. "Yes, I did."

"Then why didn't you tell me?"

He put his arm around me. "That would have kind of spoiled the surprise, don't you think?"

I nodded, overwhelmed by the emotion of the moment and very glad I hadn't known. It was an absolutely perfect surprise and the best Mother's Day gift I had ever received.

I listened as Gabriel spoke, marveling at the self-assured, articulate man he had become. I shed more tears, this time out of gratitude to God for blessing me with an amazing son.

When Gabriel finished, the pastor asked each of the other children to speak. After everyone had taken a turn, he said, "Now go to where your mother is sitting, give her a hug, and tell her how much you love her." I took a deep breath, blinked a few times in an effort to regain my composure, and looked up to see my five beautiful children standing around me. They were all smiling and looking at me through eyes that told me that I was loved and that I was a good mother. More importantly, I was their mother, and, for a few crystal clear moments, I knew, without a doubt, that they wouldn't have it any other way.

It was the best Mother's Day I'd ever had, but I couldn't help thinking about my mother. Her presence was so strong that it didn't take much for me to imagine her sitting right next to me, sharing this remarkable celebration. She was still so much a part of me and so much a part of the grandchildren she never had the chance to know. She was in Emily's eyes and in her strong, determined personality. She was in Gabriel's long, slender fingers and his love for music. So many things about the children reminded me of her.

Perhaps it was because I felt her presence so keenly that I was able to picture myself turning to her and saying, "Mom, I'd like you to meet your grandchildren."

She wouldn't be able to speak for a few moments because, like me, she'd be crying. Then she would hug me hard and whisper in my ear. "I'm so proud of you," she'd say. "You've done a wonderful job."

My mother will always be a guest of honor on Mother's Day, but yesterday I finally felt like one, too.

"Joy is prayer—Joy is strength—Joy is love—Joy is a net of love by which you can catch souls."

—*Mother Teresa*

Stopping the Clock

On the morning of my son Gabriel's birthday, I glanced at the clock on my computer. It read 11:07. With a flood of bittersweet remembrance, I realized that twenty years ago, Gabriel was approximately three minutes old.

Prompted, and then propelled, by an awesome power, he had made the perilous journey from his safe, inner world into my waiting arms. Two souls who inhabited one body for nine long months met for the first time. Two people linked by unconditional love looked into each other's eyes. Exhausted and tearful, not from my physical labors, but from the relief that he had been born whole and healthy, I marveled aloud at his presence.

I watched my husband Tom's eyes widen with disbelief and amazement. Nothing had prepared him for this moment, the birth of his first child. Not his hand on my distended stomach feeling the baby move, not his ear pressed to my skin listening to the heartbeat, not even the image of a fetus floating on an ultrasound screen. Only when he held Gabriel in his trembling, uncertain arms did he realize that there had, indeed, been another human being inside of me. One plus one now equaled three.

The sight of my son evoked a rush of tenderness and love so great it weakened me. Every moment of despair, every single terrible thing that had ever happened to me paled and lost its power.

For several days, all I had to do was close my eyes to recall the incredible sensation of his movement down the birth canal. I swore I would never forget that feeling, but it faded and left me trying to recapture it. For weeks I felt a phantom baby moving within me. That sensation also disappeared and I mourned its loss.

Tom and I discussed the birth over and over again with the zeal of the most enthusiastic Monday-morning quarterbacks. As time passed, the event took on a surreal quality, almost as if we mortals knew that our brush with the miraculous, an experience as amazing as the one we went through, couldn't possibly happen in our ordinary world.

With Gabe's birth, I swore I would make the clock tick more slowly. Each moment would be savored, every milestone recorded. Nothing would slip past me.

Nevertheless, as though anxious to reach some invisible finish line, time hurtled by. One minute I cradled my newborn son, caressing his tiny fingers, and inhaling his special scent. Then, in what seemed like only a few days, I looked up to see him toddling away from me, a cracker clutched in those precious fingers. I closed my eyes and opened them to see him riding his first tricycle down the front walk. The toddler went to bed one night and woke up as a little boy.

One evening last week, Tom and I sat in the family room and watched Gabriel putting on his jacket in preparation for an evening out with his friends. A car pulled into our yard and he waved goodbye. "I won't be late," he called as he went out the door.

"I can't believe he's twenty," Tom said, and I detected a slight quiver in his voice.

"I know what you mean," I said. "He's all grown up." I paused and grinned. "On the outside, anyway." I gave Tom a quick hug. "But he'll always be our baby. Do you remember the morning he was born?"

"Of course, I do. I couldn't believe how big he was." He laughed. "I'll never forget when you told the doctor you weren't very good at pushing."

I nodded, ready to finish his sentence. "And then three pushes later, there he was." We sat in silence for a few moments. I thanked God for my wonderful child, now a young man, and for a husband that cherished the memory of that extraordinary day as much as I did.

"The walls we build around us to keep out the sadness also keep out the joy."

—*Jim Rohn*

"May I Have this Dance?"

I have always loved to dance. My mother used to joke that I learned to dance in utero. She often sang to me while she was pregnant, and both she and my father loved music—a passion I shared from a very early age. I grew up listening and dancing to a wide variety of music that included classical, popular, and even opera. Of course, once I reached a certain age, my music interests grew to include rock n' roll, and my dancing was done with friends on Friday and Saturday nights.

Occasions for dancing dwindled as marriage and work became the focus of my life. When I became pregnant for the first time, I watched in amazement (and more than a little apprehension) as the needle on the scales kept climbing. Dancing was reduced to a fond memory.

"Everything about your life will change," a friend told me before my son's birth. I smiled and nodded as if this was something for which I was completely prepared. Secretly, I decided she was being a bit dramatic. Surely some things about my life would remain intact, I thought. It didn't take long for me to discover she had been telling the truth. I also decided she should have grabbed me by the shoulders and stared me straight in the eye to make sure I listened to every single word of her profound announcement.

Despite the changes, I fell in love with my new son and my new lifestyle. My body returned to a somewhat modified version of my pre-pregnancy days. I learned I could stay in the bath longer than five minutes and overcome the worry that my son would stop breathing, and my life was restored to something resembling a routine.

The only thing I truly missed about the old days was uninterrupted sleep. I didn't have much choice in the matter. My nights, as well as my days, had been taken over by a tiny, helpless bundle wielding absolute power. For weeks, I wandered through an exhaustion-induced fog, convinced that the person who said, "No one ever died from lack of sleep," had been childless. Miraculously, the semblance of a nighttime schedule eventually began to form, and I found myself getting up to feed the baby only once—usually about 2 A.M. My body and my mind made some adjustments, too. A more regular sleep schedule did wonders for my attitude, and I began to spend these nighttime rendezvous getting to know a very complex and interesting individual—my son.

Though they happened almost twenty years ago, I can still recall those times clearly. We'd sit in almost complete darkness, the house still and quiet around us. I'd stroke his almost nonexistent hair, trace his perfect shell-like ears, and marvel once again at his beautiful hands—so much like my mother's—and his pudgy little feet with their toes that reminded me, for some reason, of kernels of corn. One night, I realized that my son and I were not alone. We were in the company of thousands of mothers feeding and caring for their babies, each in their own blessed darkness and quiet, but all part of a special sisterhood, creating relationships that would last forever. Invariably, I'd smile and, in time, I was rewarded with a priceless gift when my son smiled back at me. Of course, we talked, although anyone observing us might think the conversation was completely one-sided. I may have been the only one using conventional words, but the baby spoke volumes to me with his eyes. It will come as no surprise to any mother that we understood each other completely.

It was about this time that music videos became popular, and I began to turn on the television softly to enjoy some music during feeding time. My love for music had never waned, but it had been a long time since I'd been able to sit and listen to any. I soon developed a liking for several of the hit songs that were in heavy rotation at that time, and one night as we sat there, I found myself feeling that once familiar urge. I looked into my son's eyes and asked, "Hey little guy, wanna dance?"

I stood up and moved around the room to the music. At first, the baby appeared a little apprehensive and I held him tighter for reassurance. His body soon relaxed and he smiled, appreciating the sensations my dancing produced. It was more than obvious to me that he was enjoying it as much as his partner. I found myself surrounded and enveloped not only by the music but also by a feeling of overwhelming and complete happiness.

I still hear those special songs sometimes, and I can't help but stop whatever I'm doing and travel back in my mind to those moments of pure joy. And yes, sometimes I even get up to dance.

"In your presence is fullness of joy."

—*Psalms 16:11*

Chapter Two
An Iris for Faith

You can't help but notice the elegant iris amongst the flowers we've gathered for our mother's bouquet. This tall, stately blossom represents faith—a noble flower to symbolize noble attributes. Remembering the fragrant blooms from childhood gardens, we grow up to plant our own elegant irises. And in the same way, as we recall the faith, we find the strength and encouragement to make our way in the world.

Faith

Your child is born with a simple, steadfast faith, a fragile seedling that must be protected and nurtured if it is to grow and set down roots that will keep it firmly in place. Watch over it with great care lest the world damage or even destroy it. Like tenacious weeds, fear and doubt will suffocate faith and thrive in its place. Resist your adult urge to complicate a pure and beautiful thing, and become like a child yourself. As your child slips his hand into yours at a busy intersection, trusting that you will lead him safely across, put your life in God's hands and believe that He will shield you from all harm.

Noah's Wife's Story

"Strength and honour are her clothing; and she shall rejoice in time to come.

She openeth her mouth with wisdom; and in her tongue is the law of kindness.

She looketh well to the ways of her household, and eateth not the bread of idleness.

Her children arise up, and call her blessed; her husband also, and he praiseth her."

—Proverbs 31:25–28

Although the lines above weren't written specifically about Noah's wife, they could certainly be used to describe her. The Bible doesn't tell us her name, but she deserves recognition and honor as a woman of great faith and great character.

Eve may have been the mother of the human race, but the responsibility for its survival rested with Noah and his devoted wife.

Noah told his wife of God's plan to destroy the earth with a catastrophic flood and of the ark God had instructed him to build. Armed with courage and determination, she vowed to support and help him in any way she could as he carried out God's plan.

Only a woman of immense, unfaltering faith could have done this. In the many, many years it took to build the ark—a vessel of enormous proportions—she would need her faith to endure the ridicule of neighbors who had never seen rain, much less the devastation of a flood. She would need her faith to dispel her own doubts and fears, and she would most certainly need her faith to raise three sons in a doomed world, while doing everything she could to prepare them for the world to come.

Children have always looked to their parents as role models, and Noah's sons were no exception. Like mothers today, Noah's wife needed to make her children feel safe and secure amidst great and possibly frightening changes. She had to instill in them the faith, hope, and courage that sustained her while trying to teach them how to live in a harsh, unforgiving world.

Even now, mothers provide the example and smooth the way when the whole family has to pack up and move to a new place. It would take a wise mother, indeed, to explain to her children that the day was coming when they would have to leave everything behind and when they and their family would be the only human beings left on earth.

Noah's wife may have found herself in a unique situation facing extraordinary challenges, but the faith, hope, wisdom, and valor that saw her through her many ordeals grace mothers all over the world.

My Own Personal Cheerleader

I had been up during the night with an upset stomach and headache, and I was exhausted. I opened one eye and wondered how long it was until naptime. I usually get up about an hour before the children, so I have a chance to really wake up and prepare myself for their onslaught at six, but when I opened my bedroom door, I could hear them, all of them and what sounded like half the neighborhood, downstairs. My hand poised on the doorknob, I entertained the appealing idea of taking a few steps backwards, closing the door and crawling back into bed before anyone knew I was up.

It was too late. I heard Owen shout, "Hey everybody, Mom's up." How did he know? I hadn't made a sound, but I wasn't surprised. Like the rest of my children, Owen possessed "mommy radar," a special sensitivity to anything I might be trying to do without interruption—leisure activities like having a bath, talking on the telephone, or sleeping. I took a deep breath and forced myself down the stairs.

Truth was, I wouldn't have stayed in bed long, anyway. My usual chores were waiting for me, and I knew countless other things needed to be done—things that I couldn't quite remember while my mind remained mired in an exhaustion-induced fog. Life was a lot more organized when I used to keep lists, but I hadn't found the time to make one since about 1994.

I had almost made it to the bottom of the steps when Owen appeared. "Hi, Mom, you slept in. Can you make me a waffle?"

I opened my mouth, but nothing came out. Obviously, my voice wasn't functioning yet, so I only nodded. Connor was next. "Mom, I need you to sign this paper, and can you make me a waffle?" I nodded again and took a few more steps. I glanced at the floor just in time to avoid stepping in a good morning offering from the dog.

Miraculously, my voice returned. "Emily," I shouted. When my daughter appeared at the top of the stairs, I explained that if I should happen to sleep in, I would greatly appreciate it if she would take the dog out.

"Oh, Mom, I need a bus note. I'm going to Lisa's house after school, remember?"

I must not be speaking English, I thought, or perhaps the stomach virus had also affected my voice. I decided that if I just kept nodding, I might make it through the morning. I gave it another try and told her about letting the dog out. "Oh, I'm sorry," she said. "I'll be down in a minute to clean it up."

Since I knew the odds were astronomical that someone else would find the dog's surprise with a foot before Emily made it downstairs, I cleaned it up myself. I finally made it to the kitchen to find Owen and Connor making their own breakfast. I knew the road to self-sufficiency was littered with pools of spilled syrup and puddles of milk, but that morning, I was low on tolerance, patience, and whatever else it took to foster their independence. The boys took one look at my face and slunk out of the kitchen.

I felt a twinge of guilt, but my fatigue had opened the door to an assortment of feelings that weren't the least bit maternal. I stared at the mess on the kitchen table while my resentment and indignation simmered and then came to a boil. My son Dylan came into the kitchen. "Good morning, Mom," he said.

"Have you done your chores?" I asked. His smile vanished, replaced by a wounded look not unlike that his two brothers had worn a few minutes earlier. He shook his head, picked up the broom and dustpan, and left the room.

I poured myself a cup of coffee. As I headed for my desk, I recalled that Dylan had a big science test that morning. He needed words of support, not demands, but I was too far gone. I had started the day's journey on a path of thoughtless words and ugly feelings and I didn't seem to be able to come to a stop and change direction. Writing bus notes, handing out lunch money and signing letters didn't help one bit. While I filled everyone's cup with strength, comfort, and encouragement to face the day, my own cup remained empty and dry.

I glanced at my computer screen and noticed an e-mail from my pastor's wife. She often sent me messages during the day. Her short, friendly notes usually made me smile, but not today. Not with the thick blanket of self-pity I had draped over my shoulders. I hit the reply button and sent her a long message describing my terrible morning. Surely, she would give me the sympathy I deserved. I wrote, "I feel like I'm everyone's cheerleader. Who's my cheerleader?"

It didn't take long for her to write back, and it wasn't the answer I expected. Her message read simply,

"Philippians 4:13.

"I can do all things through Christ which
strengtheneth me."

I had heard my pastor's wife repeat these words many times.
She had whispered them to me one Sunday at church when
I was asked to get up and speak in front of the congregation,
something I had told her I dreaded. She had been right then,
and she was right again. I did have a cheerleader. The best one I
could possibly have.

It was definitely time for some apologies, but before I
rounded up the children, I thanked God for sending me a map
and getting me back on the right road.

*"To one who has faith, no explanation is necessary.
To one without faith, no explanation is possible."*

—*St. Thomas Aquinas*

"If Mom isn't happy..."

Every Sunday, after we've had the opening prayer and sung some hymns, our pastor always asks if anyone has a blessing to share. One week, his wife raised her hand and told us that she had experienced a miracle the day before. "I went to some yard sales yesterday," she said, "and my husband actually went with me!" She grinned and gestured toward the pulpit. "He never goes to yard sales."

There was some laughter and a few teasing remarks that he must have gone because he had heard that someone was selling fishing equipment. The pastor shrugged and lifted his hands as if admitting his guilt. "You never know what you might find," he said. "But yard sales make my wife happy, and when she's happy, I'm happy." I saw several husbands, including my own, nodding in agreement. "In fact," the pastor added, "if Mom isn't happy, it affects everyone in the whole house."

A few weeks later, during our Mother's Day service, he made a similar remark. He reminded the children and fathers that mothers should be treated with love and respect all year long, not just on Mother's Day. "Besides," he said, "treating Mom well works out for everyone, because if Mom isn't happy, then no one is happy."

While the pastor continued his message, I began to think about what he had just said, and I recalled the first time he had brought it up some weeks ago. Of course, I knew I was capable of affecting those around me with my mood, but I had never realized to what extent. After remembering a few episodes when I had been in a less than pleasant mood, I had to admit he was right.

Something did happen to the rest of the family when I felt cranky and self-centered. Like a virus, my feelings contaminated anyone who had the misfortune to come into contact with me. This was a virulent and highly contagious bug, so before long, the whole family was infected, creating an unpleasant and uneasy atmosphere that had everyone feeling miserable.

I thought of the times I had been short-tempered or impatient with one of the boys, only to have to speak to him a few minutes later for being nasty or unkind to one of his siblings. The pastor hadn't mentioned animals, but there were times when even the dog and parrot picked up on my moods. The parrot would screech as though someone was strangling him, and the poor dog would slink around as if she'd been caught stealing something from the kitchen garbage.

It became obvious to me that if I could affect the mood of our home in a negative manner, then I should be able to accomplish the reverse. I knew I couldn't do it alone, though, so I turned to my enduring, infallible source of support—God. I asked Him to keep me aware of the power I had and, on those days when I forced my family to stumble around in the darkness of my bad mood, I asked him for the strength to fling the curtains open and let light fill the house.

"Now faith is the substance of things hoped for, the evidence of things not seen."

—*Hebrews 11:1*

Chapter Three

A Chamomile for Patience

Because a mother's love is infinitely patient, we must include the chamomile to represent her forbearance and steadfast resolve. This unassuming little flower is a perfect match for the countless times she faces the trials and challenges of motherhood calmly and without complaint. Don't be deceived by the simple appearance of the chamomile blossom or by the calm and stoic expression on a mother's face. The charming chamomile is a powerful herb, and mothers, as we all know, possess a formidable potency all their own.

Patience

If you can remember what it was like to be a child, you will discover a vast store of patience for your own children. Search your memory and recall the frustration, confusion, and longing of childhood. Remember the shoelace that wouldn't tie, the bike that wouldn't balance, and the endless questions that needed answers? Eventually, the shoelace stayed tied, the bike remained upright, and at least some of your questions were answered, often because your mother took the time and had the patience to keep trying. She taught you so many things, and every time she stopped to teach or help, she provided a message—"You have value, and I love you just the way you are."

Elizabeth's Story

*"And it came to pass, that, when Elizabeth heard the
salutation of Mary, the babe leaped in her womb;
and Elizabeth was filled with the Holy Ghost . . .
And blessed is she that believed: for there shall be
a performance of those things which were told her
from the Lord."*

—Luke 1:36, 45

At a time when most women her age were enjoying their
grandchildren, Elizabeth had all but given up hope of ever
having a child. She had a loving husband, Zechariah, with
whom she shared a deep faith, but there were times when the
quiet of their peaceful home deafened her and when she feared
that her failure to have a baby was a reproach from God. And
yet she waited and harbored the tiny hope that like Sarah,
Rebekah, and Rachel, women whom God had blessed with a
child in their later years, she, too, might someday cradle her own
sweet baby.

Elizabeth's patience and prayers resulted in a miracle.
The angel Gabriel appeared to Zechariah and told him that
Elizabeth would conceive a son who would grow up to become
John the Baptist, the prophet promised by God as the one who
would herald the coming of Christ.

Elizabeth's days were filled with excited anticipation as the son God had promised grew inside her. There may have been times, early in her pregnancy, when Elizabeth rested her hand on the slight curve of her stomach and wondered how an old woman like herself could possibly be having a child. After a moment, she would have shaken her head and laughed at her own foolishness, knowing in her heart that nothing is impossible with God. The angel Gabriel also paid a visit to Mary, one of Elizabeth's relatives. He brought her the unbelievable news that she, like Elizabeth, would give birth to a boy. Her child would not grow up to be a prophet like John the Baptist—he was destined to be the Messiah Himself.

When Gabriel told Mary that Elizabeth was also pregnant with a son, Mary hurried to Elizabeth's home to share the wonderful news. At the sound of Mary's greeting, the child in Elizabeth's womb leapt for joy, confirming that her most cherished dream was about to come true.

For the next three months, every movement from within would fill Elizabeth with happiness and hint at the bounty of blessings to come. Years of patience had been rewarded with one of God's greatest gifts.

Like Mother Like Son

It usually isn't until we have children of our own that we begin to appreciate what our mothers went through. Although I don't recall my mother getting angry often, when she did, even our small dog ran and hid under the bed. I remember countless hugs and few reprimands, and I'm still in awe of how deep her well of patience must have been.

Like other parents, I'm sure my mother and father waited with excited anticipation for my first word. They were delighted as my vocabulary increased, as words became sentences and then as sentences evolved into conversation and description. A trickle of words became a deluge as I realized how much I enjoyed the sound of my own voice. The verbal tap had been turned on, and my words flowed whenever I had an audience—and even sometimes when I didn't. My mother told me once that she and my father could often hear me talking to myself at night after I'd been sent to bed.

I don't recall being excessively talkative; however, I do distinctly remember what the back of the piano looked like in kindergarten. That particular spot in the room was known as "the chatterbox corner," and I spent an inordinate amount of time there.

If my mother wasn't a good listener before I came along, she soon became one. She listened and listened, and she listened some more. I'm sure that once in a while I even permitted her to contribute something to our almost exclusively one-sided conversations. And rarely, very rarely, she would become exasperated and say something like, "Do you think you might be able to be quiet for five minutes?"

I wasn't the least bit hurt or offended. Anxious to do what I'd been told, I'd find a clock somewhere and wait for five minutes. Then I'd hunt down my poor mother and start all over again.

I suspect I came by my passion for talking honestly. My mother was the sort of person who would tell her life story to someone in the grocery store, and as a child, long after I should have been asleep, I could hear my father reading and talking to my mother in their bedroom. My first four children all demonstrated their love for the spoken word, and I confess that I was a bit smug. I was surrounded by talkers, and, for the most part, it didn't bother me. Perhaps I had more patience than I thought. Then along came Owen.

For me, each pregnancy brought with it more excitement than the one before. By now, I definitely knew there would be lots of sleepless nights, plenty of frustration, and no shortage of moments when I would question my sanity. However, the enormous payoff completely overshadowed any drawbacks or deterrents there might be. I had found my niche in life. I was a mom, and I loved it.

With three older brothers, a sister, and two parents who all adored him, Owen didn't need to do much talking. There was always someone to cater to his every whim, but I wasn't surprised when, like the others, he began to talk early and often. Then, the fall when Owen had just turned three, everyone went back to school including, for the first time, my second youngest son, Connor. He had been Owen's best friend from the beginning, and the chatter of their voices and games had been the background music of my day.

Owen was lost without Connor. He'd always been a resourceful child, and I suppose he figured that he might as well find a replacement for Connor during school hours. He didn't have to look very far to find one—me.

Owen and his nonstop talking became my shadow. Sometimes, I'd stop and wonder if he was ever going to pause and take a breath. I learned to smile, nod, and make appropriate responses, but I admit there were times when I had absolutely no idea what he was talking about. It was as if a switch was turned on as soon as he woke up in the morning. His eyes would open and, within seconds, so would his mouth.

Having four older siblings had made a difference. "Listen to his vocabulary," my husband said one evening.

"You listen to his vocabulary for a while," I replied. "I'm going to hide in the bathroom for an hour." As I ran my bath water, I could hear Owen talking to me through the closed door. If I had forgotten to lock the door, he would open it just a crack. "So you can hear me better," he would say.

I often watched him sleep, amazed by how much I loved him and deeply humbled by the blessing of his very existence. He was such a sweet, funny, and affectionate little man, and I knew his nonstop chatter was a blessing in disguise, too. It reassured me that my precious boy was smart, sensitive, and full of wonder. It reminded me of how lucky I was to have the opportunity to see the world through his words.

But that didn't stop me from wishing for occasional periods of peace and quiet. I began to develop a true appreciation for my mother who had also lived with, and survived, endless conversation. So, it didn't surprise me at all when, one day, I said, "Do you think you could be quiet for five minutes?" And it came as no shock when Owen smiled, looked at the kitchen clock, and said, "Sure."

"Have patience with all things, but chiefly have patience with yourself."

—*Saint Francis de Sales*

The Patience Pin

Our congregation may be small compared to many other churches, but we are blessed with an abundance of gifted members. Our youth leader, Nathan, has gained the trust and respect of the teenagers. Thanks to him, they are learning how to follow Christ in a confusing world rife with the wrong messages. Helen, a kind, motherly lady in her seventies, could be a theology professor, and Dawn keeps us singing with her beautiful piano playing.

Every Wednesday night, while the adults meet in the sanctuary for Bible study, the youngest children spend an hour playing games and having a Bible study of their own. Dottie, a busy mother of three, puts a lot of time and effort into making this time both fun and instructive. Her enthusiasm and genuine affection for children have a lot to do with the fact that our six-year-old, Owen, loves going to church on Wednesday.

One evening, after church, Owen proudly displayed a small safety pin, strung with tiny, colored beads, attached to his shirt. "Look what we made with Miss Dottie," he said. "It's a patience pin."

I had no idea what a patience pin was, but given Owen's flair for description, I knew that all I had to do was smile and he would tell me exactly what I needed to know. So I gave him an encouraging smile and, sure enough, he kept talking. "I'm supposed to wear the pin for a whole week," he said, "and every time I look at it, I'll remember to be patient."

"That's a great idea," I said, "but why did you put beads on the pin?"

"Well," he said and paused. "I forget." A solemn look appeared on his face as he straightened his shoulders and took a deep breath. "Now I remember. The beads are for Jesus. The white one is His birth, the black one is His death, the red one is His resurrection, and the other ones mean something, too." He reached for my hand and began to lead me toward our car. "It helps you to be patient if you think of Jesus, you know. Maybe you should get a patience pin."

His comment made me wonder if my need for patience was that obvious. "Hmm," I said, "maybe I should."

Owen wore his pin faithfully all week. He refused to transfer it to another shirt or let me remove it, so the shirt and the pin went through the wash several times. He loved that pin and tried, with all the patience a boy his age could muster, to live up to its name.

The following Wednesday, when Dottie asked me if Owen had worn his pin all week, I smiled and nodded. "And he was a very patient boy, too," I said. No Academy Award–winner ever looked more gratified than Owen did at that moment.

Later that night, as he prepared for bed, I asked him if he'd like to take the pin off his shirt. He gave my offer serious consideration for a few moments and then handed his shirt to me. "You can put it on your shirt," he said.

This time I had to ask. "So you figure I could use some patience, huh?" I said in a teasing voice.

"Oh no," he said. "You're really good at patience. I just thought you might want to have it so you can look at it and think about Jesus."

I carefully removed the pin from his shirt and attached it to my own. "I'd love to think about Jesus," I said, "and even though you think I'm doing okay with patience, I could always use a little more."

Owen grinned and nodded. "Maybe just a little more," he said.

"But let patience have her perfect work, that ye may be perfect and entire, wanting nothing."

—James 1:4

Chapter Four

A Deep Pink Rose for Gratitude and Appreciation

No arrangement of flowers would be complete without a rose. For our mother's bouquet, we've selected two deep pink roses. One represents a mother's gratitude—strong, enduring feelings of thankfulness that can make her laugh, reduce her to tears, or silence her with awe. The second rose symbolizes the appreciation of her children. But how can a simple flower convey a thousand thank-yous? How can we show her how much we appreciate everything she's done? We needn't worry. A mother knows this rose is proof that gratitude has found a place in her child's heart—a message that she will cherish forever.

Gratitude and Appreciation

Remind your children to say thank-you and praise God, not just for the sandwich you made them or for the sunny weather on the day of their big game, but for the little blessings that, at one time or another, we all take for granted. Take gratitude out of the closet where you've been saving it for a special occasion and make it something you wear every day. Develop an attitude of appreciation, and your children will, too. After the bedtime story, take turns praising God; it doesn't have to be Thanksgiving to ask everyone at the dinner table to name something for which they are thankful. And while you're thanking your son for bringing up his grade in algebra or your daughter for finally cleaning up her room, don't forget to thank them for being the best thing that ever happened to you.

Hannah's Story

*"Wherefore it came to pass, when the time was
come about after Hannah had conceived, that she
bare a son, and called his name Samuel, saying,
Because I have asked him of the LORD."*

—1 Samuel 1:20

*"And Hannah prayed, and said, My heart rejoiceth
in the LORD, mine horne is exaulted in the LORD:
my mouth is enlarged over mine enemies; because
I rejoice in thy salvation. There is none holy as the
LORD: for there is none beside thee: neither is there
any rock like our God."*

—1 Samuel 2:1–2

Hannah was no stranger to the heartbreak of infertility. Despite
the love and comfort of a devoted husband, she grieved for the baby
she couldn't have and watched in torment as the women around
her gave birth and rejoiced in motherhood. With the arrival of each
new child, Hannah's feelings of isolation increased, and her sense
of purpose and identity waned.

She turned to God, not only with her desperate plea for
a child but for a source of consolation and healing for her
emotional pain. She vowed that if He blessed her with a son,
she would dedicate the child to do God's work in the temple

at Shiloh. She finished her prayer, still with no promise of a child, but filled with God's comfort and the courage to face her situation.

God answered Hannah's prayer, and she gave birth to Samuel, one of the most important prophets and leaders in the Old Testament. Her profound gratitude led to a powerful prayer of thanksgiving to God, not just for granting the desire of her heart, but for His solace and strength in the moment of her deepest misery.

Hannah kept her promise to God and when Samuel was a young boy, she took him to the temple to be raised as a man of God. Despite their separation, her devotion to Samuel never faltered. She visited him each year at the temple, bringing him a new robe—a garment crafted by her own loving hands, each stitch carrying her constant prayers for his safe-keeping and happiness. God continued to reward Hannah for her gratitude and faith with the birth of five more children.

Hannah's moving story is a powerful reminder to express our gratitude. Just as gifts can come in an endless assortment of shapes and sizes, gratitude can take many forms. Whether it's a heartfelt vow and prayer to God as with Hannah, or a simple thank you for a stranger's kindness, our thankfulness is a recognition of blessings large and small and carries with it great rewards. Just ask Hannah.

A Rare Jewel

I'm a lucky mother. My oldest son's girlfriend is a rare jewel. Jade is bright, beautiful, and sensitive. She shares Gabriel's interests and supports his hopes and dreams, but all that is simply icing on the cake, because she makes him happy.

It was Gabriel's birthday recently, and Jade sent him a large box overflowing with funny, thoughtful, and loving gifts. As I stood watching him open his packages, he handed me a tiny box and an envelope. "These are for you," he said.

"For me?" I asked in a voice full of surprised pleasure. I was moved by the fact that Jade had acknowledged me in her celebration of Gabriel's birthday, and I was reminded of a woman with whom I worked some years ago. When I told my friend it was my birthday, she asked me if I had sent my mother flowers. "Why would I send my mother flowers? It's my birthday."

My friend feigned indignation and pointed her index finger at me. "Because she gave birth to you, and she deserves to be thanked."

I phoned my mother later that day to thank her, something I continued to do every year until she died. I've always been grateful to my friend, as well, for showing me another way I could let my mother know how much I appreciated everything she had done—starting with my birth.

My son nudged me. "Open your present," he said.

Inside the tiny box was a beautiful, carved bear, hand-painted in what appeared to be a Native American design. It was within the card, however, that I found a gift I've only dreamed of receiving. I read the contents out loud to my husband, standing next to me.

"I hope this card finds you well. First off, I wanted to say that I am sending you this card to say thank-you. You have always been very kind to me and very friendly, and I appreciate it.

"Secondly, I wanted to say thank-you for giving birth to, and raising such a wonderful son. I absolutely adore him, and I hope you do, too."

The card went on to describe the gift she had sent, but my voice had become hesitant and soft as my eyes filled with tears.

"Are you crying?" Gabriel asked.

I shrugged a little and smiled. "No one has ever thanked me for that before."

"Feeling gratitude and not expressing it is like wrapping a present and not giving it."

—William Arthur Ward

Random Acts of Kindness

It may have been eighteen years ago, but I remember it as though it happened yesterday. One evening after supper, I decided to get a few groceries, and when my three-year-old son, Gabriel, discovered my plans, he begged to come along.

"Sure," I said and we headed out the door together. Once in the car, he chattered nonstop, vibrating with the excitement of someone off to his first Broadway show. When we arrived at the store, I found a cart and hoisted Gabriel into the child's seat. I didn't have much of a list, but we went up and down all the aisles anyway, going through our time-honored routine of Gabriel asking for things and me saying no.

Then suddenly, in aisle number five, right beside the juice boxes, Gabriel announced that he didn't feel very well and proceeded to vomit over the side of the cart. I stood there for a few seconds, paralyzed by astonishment, as a young couple passed our cart, giving us an extremely wide berth. "Can you imagine," I heard the woman say, "taking a young child out when he's ill like that?"

I felt my face flush and grow hot with embarrassment. Gabriel had begun to cry, and I was tempted to join him. Another cart passed us, this time pushed by a woman wearing a sympathetic smile and holding out a plastic produce bag. "Here," she said, "this might help." I flashed a weak smile of thanks and took the bag just in time for Gabriel to make use of it.

When I looked up, the woman was gone. She had been alone, but I decided that she must be a mother, and a quick-thinking one at that. With only a few words, she had managed to let me know that she understood how I felt, that I wasn't a horrible mother, and that sometimes these things just happen. It would be nice if I could have thanked her properly, because on that evening in aisle number five, she gave me a lot more than just a plastic bag.

"Courtesies of a small and trivial character are the ones which strike deepest in the grateful and appreciating heart."

—Henry Clay

Not Really Goodbye

My Aunt Charlotte never had children of her own, but from the moment I slipped into her life every summer and school holiday, I became her little girl. No daughter had parents more loving and committed to their child's well being than I did when I stayed with her and my Uncle Jack.

I spent most of my time on their farm in southern Alberta, Canada, on my own, but I rarely felt lonely or bored. Empty granaries, swept clean, became playhouses or stores, occupied by imaginary friends and customers. An ancient upright piano in the living room beckoned me to compose and produce ghastly sounds for as long as I pleased. No one ever said, "Stop that horrid racket." Slippery piles of old magazines and catalogues were the raw materials for entire towns of paper dolls.

The entire prairie waited outside for exploration and discovery. The grass crackled and broke as I walked across the yard, sending a swarm of grasshoppers into the sky. Even grasshoppers provided a source of entertainment. After capture, I took my unfortunate insect prisoners to the chicken pen and tossed them in. The chickens dashed around trying to catch the grasshoppers while I stood there, experiencing tiny flickers of remorse. Five minutes later, I would do it again.

One summer, Aunt Charlotte placed a hen and her chicks under my care, a chore I accepted with great enthusiasm. The unfriendly and ill-tempered mother hen repaid my kindness with several nasty pecks. Being responsible for her well being lost its appeal as I became increasingly annoyed by her ungrateful attitude.

One morning, while feeding her, the expression "madder than a wet hen" popped into my head. I'd heard Aunt Charlotte say this, and I decided to test the validity of those words. I poured water over the unfortunate chicken, enraging her in a very gratifying manner. But my satisfaction quickly turned into horror when the furious bird attached herself to the back of my shirt. I raced back to the house while she exacted her revenge by beating her wings about my ears and pecking me on the back of the head.

Every morning after breakfast, I took the leftover porridge to the back porch where a group of barn cats waited. Meowing and winding around my legs, the feline mob cascaded over and under each other as I poured their food into the old cast iron pot provided for them. Occasionally I missed the dish and a huge dollop of porridge landed on some unlucky cat's head.

Retreating to the cool and dark basement during the heat of the day, I spent my siestas reading the vast collection of Reader's Digest Condensed Books and Harlequin Romances that Aunt Charlotte inherited from my great Aunt Bessie when she died. Those books and my treasured comics made up the staples of my literary diet during those summers long ago.

When dark and ominous clouds gathered in late afternoon, I knew the cannons of thunder and brilliant flashes of lightning weren't far behind. The frequent power outages frightened me and, unable to sleep, I made my way to my aunt and uncle's bedroom. "Auntie, wake up," I would whisper. "I'm scared." Without a word she got up, took her pillow, and led me back to my room, where she crawled into bed with me. When she rolled over, I snuggled up to her back and fell asleep.

The years passed. My days on the farm dwindled to a few precious days each year, but my relationship with my aunt and uncle remained one of the few constants in my busy life. I had just married and started my own family when my mother died. Frightened and lonely, I clung to Aunt Charlotte—my other mother. The bond between us strengthened as we supported each other in our grief for the woman who had been my mother and Charlotte's baby sister.

Even though we were separated by a distance of almost 4,000 miles, Aunt Charlotte was always there for me. On the brilliant days of happiness and fulfillment, she increased and shared my joy, but when the clouds appeared and storms of sorrow and defeat threatened, she provided a safe haven of comfort and wisdom.

When she suddenly became ill, I panicked. She would get better, I reasoned, in a moment of calm. I refused to acknowledge that she might be leaving me.

One afternoon, I dreamed I was in her hospital room. "Is that who I think it is?" she said, and her eyes told me that it meant the world to her that I was there.

My dream was no surprise. I thought of her constantly while awake, so why shouldn't she be in my dreams, too? I wondered for a moment if the dream meant that she knew how much I wanted to be with her. If I stretched my imagination far enough, if I went back to that time to when I believed anything was possible, maybe I could believe I was really there.

Four thousand miles and a ticket that would have cost more money than I possessed prevented me from traveling to her bedside. I wanted to phone her on Sunday at five o'clock just like I did every week. We'd laugh because my card arrived before her birthday for the first time in years. When my cousin told me Aunt Charlotte was dying—"that it's only a matter of time, now"—I knew that there would be no more phone calls, no more conversations to leave me smiling and secure.

During my wait for that final call from my cousin, I thought of how I had always wanted Charlotte to see our farm. So many times, I'd pictured us driving over the hill, the big one just before you get to our place. I would watch her face carefully as she saw the dignified brick house, surrounded by countless acres of peanuts, soybeans, and cotton, for the first time.

She'd see the red outbuildings, the post-and-rail fences, and the rooster stealing cat food from the bowl on the back porch and say, "It's really lovely, dear." She'd be so happy for me. As a child, I used to wish that I could live on a farm when I grew up—a dream that became a reality. Maybe wishes did come true, so I wished Charlotte wouldn't have to leave me now. I wished for years and years more to tell her how much she means to me.

We'd marvel over the glossy green magnolia tree in the front yard and the twisted, ancient sycamore in the back. I'd show her where the floodwaters stopped their frightening crawl up our driveway after the hurricane. We'd shake our heads and smile because, with time, some things become worthy of amusement and wonder. Aunt Charlotte knew how much she meant to me; she knew this because I told her countless times. But there were things I had never told her, lessons I never thanked her for, like how she taught me to believe in myself, how she taught me that forgiveness hides in every mistake, and that everyone deserves another chance.

I also never told her that watching her with Uncle Jack taught me about love and devotion. I watched her work on the farm endless hours for endless days and learned about commitment. I watched her with friends and family and learned about loyalty. When hail destroyed an ocean of golden wheat— the entire crop—on a blistering August afternoon, she held me tight and told me everything was going to be okay. That's when I learned about faith and perseverance.

When I was a girl and the time came to leave the farm and return to my family in the city, I always cried. Our time together never lasted long enough. I had never been very good at saying goodbye, but I reminded myself that this farewell was no different than the partings of my childhood. I would see my beloved Aunt Charlotte again, and the next time, there would be no goodbyes. So, I whispered, "I'll see you again someday, Auntie. There's still so many things I want to tell you."

"I thank my God upon every remembrance of you."

—Philippians 1:3

Chapter Five

A Nasturtium for Maternal Love

The flare of vibrant color in our bouquet for Mom comes from the nasturtium, the flower chosen to symbolize maternal love. Next to the fiery nasturtium, other flowers may appear wan and insignificant in the same way other forms of love may pale when compared to that of a mother for her child. The hardy nasturtium, with its large, easy-to-handle seeds, is a wonderful choice for a child's first garden. Both the flowers and leaves are edible, making it perfectly safe, and the seeds can even be used as a substitute for pepper. It's a beautiful creation, providing both pleasure and sustenance. Just like a mother's love.

Maternal Love

Motherhood doesn't just change your way of life. It transforms your very nature. Moments of shyness and trepidation are forgotten; you are now a dragon slayer, willing to do anything to protect your child. You knew you would love your baby, but nothing prepared you for the intensity of your feelings. A mother calls it love, but she knows it's so much more, just as she knows that words are useless to explain how she feels. Rejoice in this miraculous gift from God—this love that silences you with awe and swells your heart to bursting—and know that it's only possible because He loves you.

Jochebed's Story

"Love always protects, always trusts, always
perseveres. Love never fails. But where there are
prophecies, they will cease; where there are tongues,
they will be stilled; where there is knowledge, it will
pass away . . . And now these things remain: faith,
hope and love. But the greatest of these is love."

—1 Corinthians 13:8, 13

The birth of a beautiful, healthy son should have been an occasion of great joy for the Hebrew slave woman, Jochebed, but any happiness she felt was overshadowed by a desperate fear. As she cradled her baby, she had but one goal, and that was to save him from the Pharaoh's terrible edict that all newborn male slaves must die. So she prayed, and she planned, and she trusted her God.

She hid the baby for as long as she could. When she could conceal him no longer, she made a waterproof basket, whispered a fervent prayer, and kissed her son one last time. Then she set him adrift on the Nile. It would not be difficult for any mother to imagine her heartbreak at that moment. Unable to watch the helpless baby float away, she told her daughter, Miriam, to follow the basket as it made its way down the river.

In a remarkable turn of events, the Pharaoh's daughter found the baby while bathing at the river. She claimed him as her own and named him Moses. When Miriam appeared and offered the services of a slave woman named Jochebed to nurse the baby, the Pharaoh's daughter agreed, and Miriam rushed to fetch her mother. Few emotions could rival Jochebed's feelings when she held her precious son again.

The birth of a child brings with it the birth of an intense and powerful love—a love unequaled on earth. Drawing upon strength of character perhaps unknown to the new mother before that moment, she takes a silent, solemn vow to protect her child at any cost. Just like Jochebed did. And like Jochebed, mothers still pray and plan and trust God. They send their children out into an uncertain world with the faith that God will help them keep the vow they made the day their child was born.

Ties That Bind

From the moment we enter this world, our mother's is the face we look for, the touch we long to feel, and the voice that soothes us and makes us smile. She talks to us before we even know what she's saying, and from our first word to our first heartbreak, she listens. She displays the lump of clay we make in art class as if it's a masterpiece; she makes us feel like our stories are bestsellers; and she cheers even when we come in last. From the time we are little, she is always there for us. Even if we aren't together, she carries us closest to her heart and never far from her thoughts. She can banish the most terrifying monsters and perform medical miracles with a Band-Aid or a chocolate chip cookie. When we grow older and leave home, she remains behind, but her words of encouragement, her faith in us, and, most of all, her love stay with us, no matter how far we travel from home.

That spark of love she feels before our birth grows into a flame that never flickers. She loves us even when we don't know how to love ourselves. She shares our successes, our failures, our triumphs, and our tragedies. Our tears break her heart, and our smiles light up her world. We say, "I love you, Mom," not knowing that we've given her a gift she values more than jewels. When she leaves this earth, we will stumble and fall as if we were babies learning to walk all over again. But we get up and carry on, as she has taught us. We start out as part of her, but her love remains as part of us, forever.

"Before you were conceived, I wanted you.

Before you were born, I loved you.

Before you were here an hour, I would die for you.

This is the miracle of life."

—*Maureen Hawkins*

Mother Hen

I've seen plenty of wild turkeys scattered across the fields as we've driven by, but I never had the opportunity to see one from close up until the day we were traveling along one of the back roads that lead from our farm to town. Abruptly, my husband Tom braked, and we watched as a hen turkey raced across the road. I expected him to resume driving once she safely reached the opposite side, but the car remained still. "What are you waiting for?" I asked.

He smiled and pointed to the hen. She had stopped in the ditch and I could hear her calling out repeatedly. "She's waiting for someone," Tom said, and I glanced to the other side just in time to see a line of turkey poults pouring out of the ditch and crossing the road in a frantic effort to reach their mother.

We waited for a few minutes while the babies were reunited with the hen. For some reason, though, she continued her frantic call and a few seconds later, another poult, this one all by itself, emerged from the ditch and joined the group. Only then did the mother move off into the bushes, accompanied by her family.

Astonished by what I had just seen, I turned to Tom. "Did you see that?" I asked. "It was as if she knew they weren't all there. Do you think that's possible? I mean, that she knew one was missing?"

"I suppose," he said, "but it's more likely that she heard that little guy calling out to her from the other side. So she answered him and waited for him to find her."

"That's probably it," I said, but I still liked the idea of the mother knowing that one of her poults had strayed. Then I remembered the time that one of my babies had gone missing, and I hadn't even been aware of the fact.

Tom and I were at Wal-Mart with the two youngest boys. We decided to split up. Since the boys invariably chose to stay with their father when we did this, I was surprised when Connor asked to come with me. "Sure," I said and he hurried over to stand beside me.

I took another look at my list and pushed the cart toward the women's clothing. I wandered around the store for a short while and then, suddenly, came to a dead stop in the middle of an aisle— something was missing. "Oh no," I said and broke into a cold sweat. I had completely forgotten about Connor. I whirled around to check behind me, but he wasn't there.

I ordered myself to stay calm and took a couple of deep breaths. As the knot of anxiety in my stomach grew, I scanned the area around me, and I began to pray for a glimpse of my blonde, skinny boy. There was no sign of him, but Tom appeared with our other son, Owen, in tow. "Did you hear that?" Tom asked.

"Hear what?" I couldn't hear anything but the blood pounding in my ears.

He gestured to one of the speakers in the ceiling. "I just heard the strangest announcement. The woman said, 'Susan, your son, big boy Turner, is at the ladies' fitting room.' Is she talking about Connor? Has he wandered away?"

I didn't stop to answer his questions but instead rushed straight to the women's fitting room. We had been calling Connor "Big Boy

Connor" ever since Owen was born. Apparently, when the store employee had asked for his name, he'd said, "Big Boy Connor," and she'd misunderstood.

I rounded the last corner and saw him, standing in front of the fitting-room desk, his pale face streaked with tears. With a silent prayer of gratitude, I knelt down and he charged toward me like a runner who had just spotted the finish line. He wrapped his tiny arms around my neck, and I felt his wet cheek next to mine. "Oh Connor," I whispered. "I'm so sorry."

He lifted his head and looked into my eyes. "That's okay," he said and his body trembled slightly. "I knew you'd find me. I knew you'd come."

I hugged him hard and kissed his forehead. "Well, you were right. I wouldn't have stopped looking until I found you." I paused for a moment. "I hope you know that I'd do anything for you." He grinned and nodded. "Good," I said and stood up. "Well, let's go and pay for our stuff." I began to push my cart toward the checkout but, this time, I turned around to make sure my babies were keeping up with me.

"Mother is the name for God in the lips and hearts of children."

—William Makepeace Thackeray

Lesson from an Octopus

As a new mother, I soon learned that my baby had a relatively simple, yet completely effective means of communication. I discovered that one sort of crying meant he was hungry, another let me know he was uncomfortable, and yet another informed me that, just like everyone else, he needed to be held. However, as is often the case with babies, things didn't stay simple for long.

As my children grew, there were times when I had absolutely no idea why they were crying, at least not right away. There were also plenty of occasions when I couldn't fix things with a hug and a Band-Aid. Sometimes, all I could do was let them cry and try to comfort them. Every time I watched them grieve over the death of a pet, a fight with a friend, or an unkind word from a classmate, I felt the same frustration, the same ache in my heart, and I wanted to cry, too.

The other night, I found my two youngest boys enjoying their favorite nature program on television. Connor encouraged me to sit down and watch. "You'll like this," he said. "It's about mothers." I promised to join them in a few minutes, but the show was almost over when I returned.

I immediately noticed that six-year-old Owen had moved from the floor in front of the television to the couch. Perhaps he had lost interest, I thought. "What did I miss?" I asked Connor.

Connor told me a bit about the show, and then Owen spoke up. "One of the moms was really sad," he said.

It was then I understood why he sat curled up in a corner of the couch, a subdued expression on his typically animated face. "Oh," I said. "That's too bad. Which one made you sad?"

My question opened the floodgates, and Owen began to cry. I hurried to his side, wrapped my arms around him, and began to rock him gently. "Tell me about it, sweetheart. I want to know why you're so upset."

Owen was crying too hard to talk, so Connor explained. He told me how the mother octopus laid her eggs in a cave or some other sheltered place and then guarded them until they hatched. She didn't leave for any reason, not even to eat. By the time the babies hatched, she had weakened beyond recovery, and when the young were about five days old, she died and was eaten by a large fish.

"She died for her babies," Owen said in a muffled voice as I held him tight.

For a few seconds, I didn't know what to say. I was deeply moved, not only by Connor's description, but also by a feeling I couldn't share with Owen right at that moment. I wanted to tell him that I knew exactly how that protective mother octopus felt about her babies, because I feel that way about all of my children, but I remained silent, worried that I might upset him further. Before I became a mother, I had no idea that love could be so powerful, so immense, and so painful.

I told Owen that God had created a perfect plan for every living creature. He knew exactly how long the mother octopus needed to live so her babies could grow up and have their own babies. We talked about the other animal mothers on the program and how God had arranged everything perfectly for them, too.

Eventually, Owen calmed down and even smiled. It was obvious to me that he was still sad, but there wasn't a lot more I could do besides hope and pray that someday, when I'm not there to dry his tears and comfort him, he will remember how God has a way of working everything out, even for a mother octopus.

"And the mother of the child said, As the LORD liveth, and as thy soul liveth, I will not leave thee."

—*2 Kings 4:30*

Chapter Six

A Chrysanthemum for Friendship

Because a loving mother often becomes a cherished friend, we've included the chrysanthemum in our bouquet to represent friendship. As the years go by, mother and child discover a new facet to their relationship. Their precious bond is only enhanced as they discover the joys and rewards of having a true and faithful friend. The large, brightly colored blossom of the chrysanthemum is a welcome sight in any bouquet or garden. It may just trigger some fond memories, not unlike a visit with a good friend.

Friendship

My mother wore many hats. She could be a dedicated nurse, a gourmet cook, or a riveting storyteller. Some of her hats weren't very exciting or glamorous, but she wore each one with the grace of a model and the dignity of a queen. Wearing one hat or another, she did everything she could to keep me healthy, happy, and whole, but I was left feeling as though there wasn't much I could do in return. Then, one day, I realized that my mother had yet another hat to wear, and she became my friend. It was my privilege to become acquainted with the fascinating, multifaceted woman whom, up until that point, I had known only as my mother. Finally, I had the opportunity to give her something special—a small token compared to everything she had given me. I had told her countless times how much I loved her, but it was a moment of great joy when I was able to say, "I'm so glad you're my friend."

Ruth's Story

"But Ruth replied, 'Don't urge me to leave you or to turn back from you. Where you go I will go, and where you stay I will stay. Your people will be my people and your God my God.'"

—Ruth 1:16

When Ruth, whose very name means friendship, spoke these moving words of love, she was not talking to a man, as one might think. She was speaking to another woman—Naomi, her mother-in-law. When tragic circumstances left both Naomi and Ruth widows, Naomi urged Ruth to return to her own people. Ruth refused and followed Naomi to her homeland. It wasn't just a strong sense of loyalty that led to Ruth's decision. Naomi had become much more than family. She had become a much-loved and cherished friend.

As it turned out, it wasn't just Naomi who was rewarded by Ruth's devoted friendship. Ruth, herself, found great happiness when she traveled with Naomi to Bethlehem. There, she met Naomi's kinsman, Boaz, a man intrigued and impressed by what he had heard about the remarkable friendship between the young Ruth and her older mother-in-law. In time, he married Ruth, and she gave birth to their son, Obed, great-grandfather of King David.

The friendship between mother and child enhances and strengthens a bond that has been there since before the child's birth. They each discover extraordinary qualities in the other, while renewing their appreciation for the things that they have always known. A woman you once saw only as your mother becomes someone with whom you can share your laughter, your tears, and your life. She may know you love her as your mother, but does she know that you treasure her friendship as well? Take the time to tell her all the ways in which she blesses your life. A trusted friend is a priceless gift and one of the strongest threads in the fabric of your life.

My Friend, Aunt Helen

I grew up with a mother, a father, and one older brother. The four of us lived in a modest home on a manicured lot in the middle of a big city, so a Sunday drive to my Aunt Helen's place on the outskirts of town felt like a trip to another planet. She and her husband, my Uncle Fred, lived with their six children in a house Uncle Fred had built on a few acres just outside the city limits.

Everything at Aunt Helen's was as different as it could be from my customary world, organized and orderly, where my brother and I had our own bedrooms, and which my mother was very particular about keeping clean and tidy. As soon as I stepped out of the car, I was surrounded by cousins. Rambunctious, boisterous cousins who shared crowded, chaotic bedrooms and who always appeared to be involved in some kind of adventure, one that usually involved getting extremely dirty or wet.

One day, I walked into the kitchen and found my younger cousin, Jeanie, baking a chocolate cake without an adult in sight. I looked at the mess of flour and chocolate batter, covering every inch of counter space and most of Jeanie's face, and shuddered. When Aunt Helen arrived in the kitchen, I wanted to fade into the wallpaper or cover my head with my hands for protection from the explosion I knew must be forthcoming. "Oh, Jeanie," Aunt Helen said, "you made a cake for lunch today. What a good idea!"

I was highly skeptical. No one made that kind of mess and avoided trouble—not where I came from. It didn't take me long to realize that Aunt Helen was sincere, both that morning in her kitchen and at other times like it. In the years I spent visiting her home, I never saw her become impatient or upset, and I don't recall ever hearing her raise her voice. She was like my father in that respect—after all, she was his older sister.

I always enjoyed my visits, but when my father called out that it was time to go, I never argued or fussed to stay longer. I longed for my little bedroom with all my toys arranged just so, with the vanity table my mother had made from old orange crates, and my cozy bed with three pillows. Most of all, I looked forward to a bedtime story read by my quiet, gentle father and a goodnight kiss from my own sweet mother, both of whom I adored. Of course, it never occurred to me that, with only two children, my mother didn't face quite as many housekeeping challenges as Aunt Helen.

When we moved to the West Coast, I didn't see Aunt Helen for a very long time. Then she and Uncle Fred retired and moved within a few short blocks of my parent's house. I was married and busy with children of my own by that time, so our visits were infrequent and far too short. As the years passed, my mother and Uncle Fred died. Aunt Helen moved to a city where she could be close to two of her married daughters.

A few years ago, my brother urged me to get in touch with Aunt Helen. "She asks about you all the time," he said. "Write her a letter or give her a call."

It wasn't a lack of affection or desire that had prevented me from contacting her. Five children, a farm, and a quirky old house with a multitude of problems all kept me going all day and sometimes longer. My childless brother living in his apartment just didn't understand the demands constantly being made of my time. "I'm so busy," I said and remembered Aunt Helen and her six children. Something told me that she could relate to my situation.

There was a long silence. "Okay," my brother finally said. "Well, try to call her sometime, anyway. Even for a few minutes. I know it would make her happy."

Trust my brother to say that thing about making her happy, I thought. He hadn't been my brother for forty years for nothing. He knew that would get me to call.

I phoned the following Sunday afternoon and, as my brother predicted, Aunt Helen was delighted to hear from me. "I've always loved you like one of my own," she said, "and I don't want to lose you."

I had never doubted that Aunt Helen loved me, but I hadn't realized how much I really meant to her. She had just given me a priceless gift, one I would always cherish.

"I feel the same way," I said, and I meant every word. There was nothing I could do about the time I had wasted by not calling, but I could stay in touch now.

Our conversations over the next few months renewed the loving relationship I remembered so well, but they also led me to the discovery of a new friend. Not only did Aunt Helen listen to every word I said, she made me feel as though I really had something worth saying.

I loved it when she talked about raising my six cousins. I heard heartwarming, hilarious, and moving stories that always made me, with my own five children, feel as though there was finally someone who truly understood the blessings and trials of having a large family.

During one of our talks, I shared my frustration of trying to keep my house clean. I complained that I couldn't keep anything looking nice with the kids around. "Owen's moved half of his things into our bedroom, Connor's science experiments are all over the dining-room table, and we need a new couch in the playroom again." "It really doesn't matter," she said in a kind voice. "Enjoy your children as much as you can. It won't be long until your house is neat and tidy again, and you'll find yourself missing the mess, and the noise, and everything else that went along with having all those kids."

I recalled the chaotic, disorganized house I had visited as a child, and then I thought of the meticulously tidy home I had seen when I went to see Aunt Helen after Uncle Fred's funeral. "You really enjoyed your kids when they were young, didn't you?" I said.

"I certainly did," she said. "I didn't care about the mess—most of the time, anyway. I wanted to spend time with my children, and I've never regretted my choice. I had years to clean up after they all moved out. Too many years."

"And now you have grandchildren," I said.

She laughed. "And more messes to clean up. I love it."

When my first child was born, I was warned that the years would pass by like days and that he would be grown up before I realized what had happened. I looked at the tiny baby in my arms and wondered when he would sleep through the night. It didn't seem possible that he would ever be more than he was right at that moment.

That baby was now a man, and my youngest boy was ready to start school. Where had the time gone? And how much of it had I spent worrying about keeping my house clean? I ended my visit with Aunt Helen that day with a lot on my mind. My son, Owen, burst into the room, full of excitement. "Hey, Mom, do you want to help me collect eggs? I want to show you the bird's nest I made out of mud."

I glanced at the mountain of laundry sitting in the middle of the hallway, waiting for me to take it downstairs. It wasn't going anywhere, but I was. "Sure," I said, "Let's go get the eggs, and I'd love to see your nest."

"Friendship is the inexpressible comfort of feeling safe with a person, having neither to weigh thoughts nor measure words."

—George Eliot

Unbreakable

The other day, I was sitting at my desk when I heard a
horrendous crash, a terrifying noise that had me on my feet
in a heartbeat, hurrying to see what had happened. It was the
unmistakable sound of glass breaking, however, which brought
me to an abrupt halt. Suddenly, I wasn't sure this was something
I wanted to see.

Two of my teenagers, Gabriel and Emily, were already at
the scene when I arrived in the living room, their stricken faces
telling me everything I didn't want to know. A glance at the
wall explained the crash. A shelf containing dozens of treasures,
most of them once belonging to my mother, had fallen when
the shelf's hangers had pulled away from the plaster. I stood
there staring at the wall, unable to force my eyes to the floor.

When I finally looked, my worst fears were realized. Pieces
of broken figurines and other mementos littered the floor. I
could feel Gabriel and Emily waiting for my reaction. I heard
a small voice telling me to behave in an adult, rational manner
and to stay calm and be sensible about the whole thing. That
voice was quickly silenced by my emotional side when I burst
into tears and left the room.

Gabriel followed me and offered what comfort he could.
"Please don't be upset," he said. "It's not as bad as it looks. Some of
the things can be fixed. Please don't cry."

Still crying, I returned to the living room where Emily was doing her best to clean up and collect the broken pieces. She repeated her brother's attempt to console me. "Look," she said and held up a cup and its broken handle. "This isn't bad at all. It can be fixed."

I felt as though a self-centered, spoiled child had taken control of both my actions and my words. "You don't understand," I said to them. "These things belonged to your grandmother. They were perfect." I almost added, "Just like your grandmother." Thank God I didn't. My mother hadn't been perfect, and she would have laughed out loud if I had even suggested it.

I returned to the chair in front of my computer. I had managed to stop crying, but I felt horrible. Self-pity now added to the growing list of less than admirable qualities I had been demonstrating. I began thinking about my mother and how much she had loved those treasures and how pleased I was when I took possession of them after she died. I started crying again, but this time my tears weren't for things, but for a real person— a real person I missed every single day and whom I needed desperately right that minute to make everything okay.

What would she have told me if she had been there? She would have told me they were just things and things didn't matter— people did. I was quite sure she would have told me how happy she and my father were when they first got married and lived in two small rooms attached to the country schoolhouse where my father taught. I would have heard the story of the mixing bowls and the kitchen table and chairs that my father bought for her from his first paycheck, a fact that ensured their position as her most treasured possessions. It wasn't just the words I wanted to hear. I ached to hear her beautiful, confident voice, a voice that told me that she believed everything she said. I had believed those things at one time, too, but had lost sight of them in my misguided notion that it was the treasures and mementos that kept her memory alive.

I had been so wrong. It wasn't the things themselves but the stories connected to them that made them special. The exquisite yellow-and-gold cup and saucer was broken, but nothing had happened to the memory of my mother taking a sip from the cup and saying, "I don't know how you do it, but your tea always tastes better than mine."

Several of my Beatrix Potter figurines had been damaged, but I remembered each and every birthday and Christmas on which I received them. I am quite sure my mother enjoyed watching me open those gifts as much as I loved getting them. "I miss you so much," I whispered. "I'm sorry." I had forgotten one of the most important things she taught me. Worse yet, I had selfishly made my children feel inadequate and hurt their feelings. I prayed for a few minutes, asking God for His forgiveness, too. Funny thing about God and my mother—both of them have always forgiven me.

I returned to the living room, this time with what I hoped was the right attitude. "We're not going to vacuum until we're absolutely sure we have every piece," Gabriel said.

I smiled. "Sounds like a plan," I said. "I really appreciate your help." I paused for a moment. "I'd like to apologize for the way I acted and what I said earlier. It wasn't fair. You all know how much I miss your grandmother. You were just trying to help."

I could see the relief on their faces. "We can fix some of them," Emily said. "I'm sure we can."

I shook my head. "It doesn't matter. They're just things. That's all. They don't matter." I gave Emily a hug. "But people do." I picked up my Peter Rabbit figurine, looking somewhat forlorn without his big floppy hat. "They're still treasures, no matter what kind of shape they're in," I said. "And they always will be."

"Greater love hath no man than this, that a man lay down his life for his friends."

—John 15:13

Chapter Seven

A Purple Hyacinth for Sorrow

When a mother opens the door of her heart to welcome joy, she runs the risk of finding sorrow waiting there, as well. In the language of flowers, a purple hyacinth represents sorrow. We've placed this somber yet dignified bloom in our bouquet to acknowledge and honor the mothers who have faced their sorrows with courage and learned to smile again, despite an empty space in their heart.

Sorrow

It's written in fine print at the bottom of the invisible contract, the one you sign with your heart on the day your child is born. Exquisite, electrifying joy is guaranteed, but inevitably, so is sorrow. Bathed in the bliss of holding her new baby, a mother may acknowledge the possibility of sorrow, but could she possibly acknowledge its certainty? She stares in amazement at her baby's fist, clenched so tightly it could be holding the very secret to life. She carefully pulls one finger back and grins with delight when the finger returns to the fist as though held in place by a spring. She shudders at the thought of anything terrible happening to this precious new part of herself and resolves that nothing will. A mother's sorrow can take many forms and, valiantly, she often keeps her sadness hidden, to protect those around her.

There is One, however, that knows her anguish better than she knows it herself. God holds the broken-hearted in His arms until they know peace, and He promises all sorrowing mothers that joy, brilliant and true, will return—made sweeter by the days spent in sorrow's darkness.

Eve's Story

"Unto the woman he said, 'I will greatly multiply thy sorrow and thy conception; in sorrow thou shalt bring forth children.'"

—Genesis 3:16

"And Adam called his wife's name Eve; because she was the mother of all living."

—Genesis 3:20

You might say Eve had it all. She lived in Paradise at peace with her God, her husband, and her surroundings, wanting for nothing. Her constant companions were pleasure and happiness. The depression, anxiety, fear, guilt, bitterness, and envy that plague so many earthly people were strangers to her and Adam.

But in the way it so often happens even today, it only took a moment for everything to change. When Eve listened to Satan and doubted her God, sorrow—once a stranger, now an intruder—made its dark presence known. After she and Adam were banned from Paradise and the presence of God, she gave birth to two sons, but the joy that accompanied their arrival was short-lived when she was forced to face the death of one son at the hand of the other. As countless women have proven through the ages, sorrow is no match for the human spirit. We may stumble through life for a while, numbed and blinded by grief, but in time our path straightens, and our step becomes more confident and sure. Our senses return and we see the sunshine, feel the rain, and taste our tears. Memories visit as old friends, and one morning we wake up amazed and grateful—happy to be alive.

Eve went on to have two more children. Carrying the scars of sorrow, her joy this time was sweeter, more brilliant, and more precious. We have all been wounded by sorrow and carry our own scars, but like Eve, when happiness returns to our life, we welcome it, embrace it, and thank God.

A Mother's Tears

Nobody told me there would be so many tears. When my son was born, I shed tears of gratitude and relief. I stared at the miraculous bundle in my arms and thanked God for His gift. So this is what it feels like to be part of a miracle, I thought.

When he was a baby, I cried when he cried, his inconsolable sobbing filling me with both shame and fear. I'm a terrible mother, I thought. I should know what to do.

Years later, when smiles and gurgles of delight became an overflowing well of words, he said, "You're the best mom I ever had." Tears of joy filled my eyes, and I held him close. "I'm the only mom you've ever had, you silly goose," I said and held him tighter.

When he came home in second grade, carrying only two Valentine's Day cards, and said, "I don't care. It doesn't matter," I felt his pain and cried his tears for him. The ones that stung his eyes—the ones he refused to admit were there.

When a disagreement briefly clouded our love and angry words passed between us, I cried. When he apologized five minutes later and hugged me hard, I cried again.

When illness threatened to take him from me, I fell to my knees in desperate prayer and wept bitter, frightened tears. His recovery transformed my pleas to praises and my tears of sorrow to those of joy.

Thousands of days and millions of tears from the moment our eyes first met, I sat at the top of the bleachers on a high school football field and watched my son, now a young man, stride across the grass to accept his diploma. "Promise me you won't cry," he had said earlier that day, and then shook his head as if recognizing the folly of his words. "I know you'll cry," he said. And I did.

I may not welcome the tears or even know, sometimes, why I cry, but I do know the tears are part of who I am and one reason I'm the best mom my son ever had.

"Although the world is full of suffering, it is also full of the overcoming of it."

—Helen Keller

The First Goodbye

Every summer our church sponsors a weeklong camp in northern Virginia. Much like Christmas, plans and preparations begin months before the actual event, and discussions for next year's camp often start the day our church bus returns full of tanned and tired children. For several years, our three middle children, Emily, Dylan, and Connor have come home with their stories, crafts, photos, and endless bags of dirty laundry. I look forward to the relative peace and quiet of dealing with only two children instead of five, but by the time a week has passed, I find myself longing for the comforting chaos of a full household.

Last year, there had been some discussion as to whether our youngest child, Owen, should join his siblings for his first camping experience. Owen ended the debate quickly by announcing that he didn't want to go. I was secretly relieved. He's too young to be away from home for an entire week, I told myself. Truth was, I couldn't imagine being separated from him for that long. Filled with confidence that we would both be ready for camp the following summer, I gratefully accepted my reprieve.

One Sunday in spring, our pastor announced that camp was only a few months away. He looked straight at Owen and smiled. "Are you going to come with us this year?" he asked.

I was a bit surprised when Owen grinned and nodded. "Good for you," the pastor said in a voice full of enthusiasm. "You're going to have a wonderful time."

Owen looked up at me and his grin widened. "I'm going to camp," he whispered.

"That's great, honey," I said. Of course he's going to camp, I thought. Why wouldn't he go?

Later that afternoon, Owen and I went outside to water the chickens and collect the eggs. "Who's going to help you with the chickens when I'm at camp?" he said.

I put my egg basket down and put my hand on his shoulder. "Honey, you don't have to worry about that. Maybe Gabe can help. Or your dad. Maybe I'll do it myself."

Owen didn't say anything, but his brow remained furrowed as he picked up the hose and began to fill a bucket. Just before bedtime, he came into the playroom where I was watching television. "I'm not going to camp this year," he said. "I'll go next year."

"That's fine," I said. "You can go this year or next year—whatever you want. But please don't worry about it, okay?"

These scenes were repeated many times in the weeks that followed. When the subject of camp came up at church, Owen would invariably say he was going. Later, he would retract his statement, citing some excuse as to why he couldn't go. I rode the roller coaster of indecision right beside him, and there was a part of me that wanted to say, "Oh, for Pete's sake, just make up your mind!"

And then, miraculously, Owen appeared to decide. He had chosen not to go, and in the final frantic days before the children's departure, he remained true to his decision. Although I was pleased by the prospect of not having to endure an entire week without him, my conscience began to raise some annoying objections to my less than selfless attitude. I knew he would miss his brother, Connor, terribly. I knew he would have a fantastic time at camp, and if he did have the occasional bout of homesickness, he would have more than enough comfort. And if he became really upset, we could easily drive up and get him.

Maybe I should tell him these things and encourage him to go, I thought. It was then that I realized Owen wasn't the one with the problem. I was. The thought of him leaving for a week brought tears to my eyes and a familiar weight of sorrow to my heart. At first, I didn't understand why something as simple as a trip to camp was affecting me so deeply. I had been through all this with Owen's four siblings.

But Owen was my baby—at least in my mind he still was. I wasn't ready for this goodbye because I knew that it was only the first of many. It was the first of countless steps he would take before he was ready to face the world on his own. It had never been this hard before, though, perhaps because there had always been someone waiting in the wings. While the other children's growing independence had excited me and filled me with a sense of accomplishment, I now found myself feeling a bit lost and scared.

I suspected Owen wanted to go but, like me, he needed a little push, accompanied by a lot of love and support. About a week before camp, Emily and Dylan went shopping for supplies, and with a flash of insight, I gave them a list for Owen, too. There wasn't anything on the list that would be wasted if he stayed home, and I thought the sight of his own camping stuff might be the encouragement he needed. Owen took one look at his new Power

Rangers sleeping bag and Spiderman swimming shorts and began talking about all the fun he was going to have at camp. He never looked back, and when the bus pulled out of the church parking lot on its way to camp, he was in the seat right behind the driver, smiling and waving goodbye.

I managed to make it to our car before I burst into tears, and during the first few days, I missed him more than I had ever imagined. I discovered I was in good company, however, when I found my husband, Tom, looking at pictures of Owen on his computer.

When Owen returned, I asked him if he had missed us. "Of course I did," he said with a hint of indignation. "But I knew it wasn't for very long, and I'd see you soon." He wrapped his arms around my waist in a tight hug. More important than needing me, that hug told me how much he loved me. In the years to come, his needs would change, but the love would remain constant.

"Hey," he said, "did you know that it's almost the first day of school?"

I threw up my hands in mock horror. "Oh no!" I said. "Not the first day of school?"

Owen laughed. "You'll be all right, Mom," he said. "I get to come home every afternoon."

"...weeping may endure for a night, but joy cometh in the morning."

—Psalms 30:5

Chapter Eight
A Pink Carnation for Remembrance

We've chosen the long-lasting, fragrant pink carnation to symbolize remembrance. Few things are more precious to a mother than her memories. She may have photographs and other mementos to mark the steps of her journey, but her memories hold the moments that cannot be captured on film or preserved in a scrapbook. And when our mother's journey comes to an end, it is the powerful, often bittersweet memories we created together that keep her alive in our hearts. Faces may fade and voices may dim, but memories are forever.

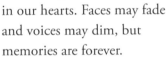

Remembrance

If I wander down the path of remembering my mother, I can be gone for hours. There are days when I feel like the road stretches on forever because so many things remind me of her. I like to take my time and make a lot of stops along the way. Sometimes I laugh, and sometimes I cry, but I always end my journey thanking God for giving me just the right mother.

A song comes on the radio, and I remember her singing while she washed the dishes. I see a waffle iron in the store, and I can taste the blueberry waffles she made for special breakfasts. I listen to my son saying the blessing at dinner, and I recall the words to the first prayer she taught me. I look at her engagement ring and smile because I never got tired of hearing the story of how she met my father. Her handwriting on a recipe card reminds me of the countless meals she cooked and the countless meals we enjoyed as a family.

It is my turn to create memories for my five children. I'd like them to remember the things I've tried to teach them and the fun times we've had as a family, but most importantly, I'd like them to remember that I loved them more than anything else in my life. Just like my own mother loved me.

Lois and Eunice's Story

"I have been reminded of your sincere faith which
first lived in your grandmother Lois and your mother
Eunice and, I am persuaded, now lives in you also."

—II Timothy 1:5

The apostle Paul was speaking to his young protégé, Timothy, when he wrote these words. It's obvious from this and other scripture that Paul had great affection for his "spiritual" son. He also had enough confidence in his trusted companion's remarkable abilities to leave Timothy in charge of the fledgling churches in Ephesus and Asia Minor.

Lois and Eunice are mentioned only once in the Bible, but their brief appearance contains a reassuring message for mothers *and* grandmothers. In many passages of scripture, Paul acknowledges Timothy's powerful faith, but here, he gives credit to Timothy's grandmother and mother for the part they played in creating, nurturing, and raising up an honorable man of God.

It's clear from the record of Timothy's life that these two women had a profound and lasting effect on him. More importantly, it's obvious that he never forgot them. He remembered their actions, their words and, most of all, their love. For without love, actions are meaningless gestures, and words are just sounds.

Paul makes no mention of the two women's status in life or of their wealth of worldly possessions. Instead, he emphasizes their passionate faith—an intangible quality that cannot be owned and that no amount of money can buy.

Our gifts from birthdays and holidays past may be forgotten, but Paul's praise for Lois and Eunice should help us remember one thing. The qualities and values we tried so hard to instill, the life lessons we struggled to teach, sometimes despairing that our children learned anything at all, remain. Like the color of their eyes, or the size of their hands, these things have become part of them. We might not witness the results of our hard work and devotion, but as the years go by, the beauty and quality of our teachings will be reflected in the kind of people our children become.

The Glue That Holds It All Together

I didn't realize it until my mother died. I didn't realize that her unconditional love and unwavering devotion to our family endowed each of us with a powerful sense of purpose and meaning. Her desire for our highest good inspired us to set goals and meet them. When she encouraged us to see the value within ourselves, she led us to recognize the value in others and in the world around us. She became an integral part of who we were, and her subtle, yet profound, teachings endured long after my brother and I left home to start families of our own. She was our constant. She was the glue that held us all together.

My father, brother, and I went out into the world each day, appearing on stage in our respective roles, but it was my mother, working behind the scenes, who directed us and made us stars. When we received a standing ovation, it was her cheers we heard first, and if we faltered and forget our lines, she was there to guide us. As is often the case when someone performs a task with great skill, she made it all look so easy.

My father may have been the one who worked outside the home, but it was my mother who gave him the confidence and courage to carry on, day after day, for forty years. It may have appeared that he made the major decisions in our family, but it was her opinion that he valued the most. In the months following her death, he shared these things and many others with me as we all struggled to find our way.

In her quiet, unassuming way, she made our home a sanctuary, a welcoming haven where she treated us like honored guests. Like any family, we weathered our share of storms—disagreements, minor rebellions, and even brief wars—but when the sun came out again, we emerged, not tattered and defeated, but stronger and more resilient.

It's only now, looking back, that I can see the way she made it all come together and how she held it all in place. We have an ancient, enormous sycamore in our backyard that reminds me of a family tree, where each member's name is written on a branch that spreads upward and splits into a multitude of tiny branches, each with its own name. The trunk reminds me of my father, strong and stable, enabling the branches to thrive and grow. And my mother? Well, you can't see her, because it's her roots that make everything possible.

"It is not how much we do, but how much love we put in the doing. It is not how much we give, but how much love we put in the giving."

—Mother Teresa

The Clown Doll

He was just an old and very decrepit clown doll, but when I was a little girl, he had a place of honor in my bedroom and in my heart as my favorite toy. My devotion to him had taken its toll. His painted, plastic face was cracked in several places, injuries I had tried to repair with Band-Aids. His shiny, satin clown suit was threadbare and torn, and his cotton stuffing had begun to leak from these holes at an alarming rate. He had a red wooden nose, which, when turned, had once played a lullaby. Now Clowny was silent, but I didn't care. When I cuddled up to him at night, I could still hear his sweet song playing in my mind.

One morning, I got out of bed and picked Clowny up from the floor where he had fallen during the night. My heart sank when I realized that his arm was close to falling off and that his suit had several new holes.

Suddenly, I knew what to do. I grabbed Clowny and hurried down the hall to my parent's bedroom, where I found my father getting ready for work. Just as I was about to ask him where Mom was, she came into the room and I handed her the doll. "Mom, can you fix Clowny?"

She stared at the doll for a few moments. "I don't know, sweetheart. He's in pretty rough shape."

"Poor old guy's falling apart," my father said, and I winced. "Maybe you should just put him away somewhere," he added. "So he doesn't get any worse."

"Put him away?" I said. "You don't mean throw him out?"

"Oh no," my father said hastily. "I didn't mean that at all."

I wasn't convinced. My father wasn't being unkind, but I knew he didn't really understand about clown dolls and other such things. "You won't throw him out while I'm at school, will you?"

My mother put her arm around me. "No, of course not. I'll see what I can do for Clowny, okay? Now, get ready for school."

Distracted by school, I didn't give Clowny much thought, but at the end of the day, I remembered my mother's promise and hurried home. She smiled as I came in the door and answered the question she saw in my eyes. "He's on your bed," she said. "I did the best I could."

At the door to my room, I stopped and my mouth fell open in amazement. Clowny wore a brand new suit, made from the same fabric my mother had used to make my clown costume for Halloween. She had even made a beautiful red ruffle to go around his neck just like the one I wore with my suit. She had washed his face and replaced the old, sticky Band-Aids, and when I peeked under his new suit, I saw neat stitches where the holes had been.

My mother appeared in the doorway. "Is that a bit better?" she asked.

I couldn't stop smiling. "Oh, thank you," I said. "He's perfect. Just perfect."

I still have Clowny. He has kept his place of honor all these years, and every time I look at him, I think of my mother and how she must have spent the whole day giving him a new lease on life. I'm sure she had things that needed to be done and other things she would have rather been doing, but she spent the day making me happy.

Many people had received gifts of my mother's exceptional handiwork, but I was the lucky recipient of one of her most precious offerings—her time spent in a labor of love.

"Good parents give their children Roots and Wings. Roots to know where home is, wings to fly away and exercise what's been taught them."

—Jonas Salk

My Mother's Hands

When I was very young, I thought my mother's hands were magical. I could give her an apple and a paring knife and, within minutes, she would present me with four delicious pieces, core removed. I couldn't tell you how she did it because, like a magician's trick, it all happened so quickly. When my brother and I played cards, all I had to do was find my mother and ask, "Can you fix my hand, please?" and she would take my slippery, disorganized pile and create a beautiful fan of cards just like my brother's.

In the evening, when we all watched television, it was as if those hands took on a life of their own. While her eyes remained fixed on the screen, her hands would be mending socks, knitting scarves and sweaters, or patching my brother's blue jeans. I was convinced my mother could do just about anything, and I believed her hands held the secret.

As I grew older, I realized that the real magic lay not in the hands themselves but in their touch. My mother filled my ears with spoken words of love, but it was her touch that sealed those words forever in my heart. It was her gentle hand on my feverish forehead that calmed and cooled me. It was her fingers, gently wiping the dirt from a scraped knee that made me forget how much it hurt. And it was her arms wrapped around me that brought comfort and healing to my aching heart.

One afternoon when I was just a little girl, my mother and I went shopping. She had become annoyed with me for some reason, and we left the store. As we walked down the street, I began to swing my arm, hoping it would bump into her and alert her to the fact that I was unhappy because I had upset her. My arm brushed her coat several times, but I was too small to make much of an impact. She didn't look down, but kept walking, eyes straight ahead. I was miserable.

Finally, I called out to her. "Mommy, please hold my hand." I had to repeat myself several times, but finally she looked down, and her face relaxed into the gentle, sweet smile I knew so well. She stopped and leaned toward me. "What did you say, sweetheart?" she asked.

I was close to tears by that time. "I want you to hold my hand. Please?"

"Of course, I'll hold your hand. And don't be sad. I'm sorry I was cross with you." Her hand slipped into mine like a whispered promise—"I will always love you."

If I want to picture my mother's hands, all I need to do is look at my own. But it's when I touch my son's cheek or stroke my daughter's hair and see the love in their eyes that I thank God for giving me magical hands, too.

"Remembering without ceasing your work of faith, and labour of love, and patience of hope in our Lord Jesus Christ, in the sight of God and our Father."

—*1 Thessalonians 1:3*

Epilogue

Closing Thoughts about Motherhood

- There is no such thing as a Super Mom. There are, however, women who appear to do it all and have it all. Truth is, they can't and they don't.
- Motherhood is not a competition. Don't let anyone make you feel inferior because you bottle-feed your baby or because he's still in diapers at age three. No schedule or timetable ever took into account the fact that every baby is an individual.
- There are good mothers who stay at home with their children, there are good mothers who return to work when their baby is six weeks old, and there are good mothers who get a job when their child starts school. They're all good mothers because they're doing what's best for themselves and their baby.
- When you're looking for good parenting resources, don't forget yourself. God gave you good instincts. Use them and trust them. Speaking of God, He's the best parenting resource or any other kind of resource in the Universe.
- Don't let guilt get the upper hand. Either use it to do things a little differently next time, or tell it to get lost.
- Don't be so hard on yourself. You weren't perfect before you had children, so why would you be perfect now?
- Making sacrifices is part of being a mother, but when you don't do anything for yourself, you risk giving your children the message that mothers don't have needs. Don't forget to say, "This is for me" once in a while.

- If you've had a particularly rough day, wait until your child goes to bed, and then watch him sleep. You won't remember the rough day, but you will remember what his face looked like while he slept.
- Make plans to take child-free breaks with your husband, your friends, or by yourself. Expect to miss your children most of the time you're gone.
- When God gave you a child, he put you in charge of a miracle. Don't forget to thank Him—often. He likes regular updates, too, so stay in touch.

Appendix

Biblical Mothers

Chapter One:
Biblical Mother: Mary (mother of Jesus)

Chapter Two:
Biblical Mother: Noah's Wife (mother of Shem, Ham, and Japheth)

Chapter Three:
Biblical Mother: Elizabeth (mother of John the Baptist)

Chapter Four:
Biblical Mother: Hannah (mother of Samuel)

Chapter Five:
Biblical Mother: Jochebed (mother of Moses)

Chapter Six:
Biblical Mother: Naomi (mother-in-law of Ruth)

Chapter Seven:
Biblical Mother: Eve (mother of all humanity)

Chapter Eight:
Biblical Mother and Grandmother: Eunice and Lois (mother and grandmother of Timothy)